Praise for Living the Abundant Life

"*Living the Abundant Life* is a must read. It is a call to action. The book is a riveting guide and full of life applications. In the book, Sylvia explains how a person can rise from poverty to prosperity. Sylvia starts off by letting the reader know how her journey from the streets of Louisiana to Detroit, Michigan led her on the road to success. She talks about how her Aunt Gladys helped her as she matriculates through college and obtained her degrees. Sylvia talks about nine principles of being successful. Seeking help from others was one of the principles. *Living the Abundant Life* is a guide to help people to navigate through the difficulties of life and to become successful."

—Minister Earline D. Vaughn, Detroit, MI

"I highly recommend reading *Living the Abundant Life*. It captivated my attention from her childhood living with her parents, living in Detroit with her Aunt Gladys, her education, working, living on her own to marriage, and on how to stop living from poverty to creating a life of prosperity. Reading this success story of her life will encourage and motivate others to start making a difference in their own life. The nine principles should be platinum and referred to as often as necessary. The book is life changing and the principles are there to guide you through. You can live an abundant life."

—Beverly F. Harris, Louisiana

LIVING THE Abundant Life

LIVING THE
Abundant Life

9 Principles to Move from Poverty to Prosperity

SYLVIA O'CONNOR

ISBN (paperback): 979-8-9879232-0-7
ISBN (ebook): 979-8-9879232-1-4

Cover photo: © Tim Babin Portraits
Book design: Christy Day, Constellation Book Services

Printed in the United States of America

Dedication

To my aunt, Gladys Coles, I will be forever grateful for all your help in guiding me and supporting me financially as I was continuing my education and career endeavors. I am also thankful for you allowing me to move to Detroit with you to make all of this happen.

Contents

Introduction

Moving on is not always easy. Whether you're moving on from a location, relationship, career, or something else, it's often a challenge. However, you never will know what is on the other side of moving on until you do it.

I am the youngest of five siblings born to a mom and dad who did not finish high school. We grew up in poverty and moved a lot growing up. I was always embarrassed by the small shotgun houses that we lived in. I had an aunt who would come to visit us every year from Detroit, Michigan. As a child, I remember her looking pretty and happy all the time. She was a Christian lady and always talked about God. When I graduated from high school, I did not have anyone to really look up to, so I turned to self-guidance to figure out what I wanted to do with my life.

I started out by going to a business college, to study office administration. One of the assignments was to write a letter to someone and mail it to them. I thought about my aunt who lived in Detroit, and in the letter I told her that I wanted to come and live with her; that I was tired of my living situation and wanted to do better in life. I really did not think she would answer me back, but she did eventually respond to my letter, and I told my mom that I was going to Detroit. I don't think my mom thought I was serious because I had never been outside of the state of Louisiana. I had started telling my friends, "I am going to Detroit."

I finally got a one-way Greyhound bus ticket to move to Detroit. We never had a car, so I do not remember which one of my uncles took me to the bus station with my footlocker. I cried like a baby on that almost two-day trip to Detroit. It would turn out to be one of the best decisions I've ever made. That was the first step on my journey to seeking a better life. When I got there, my aunt told me that she was willing to help me to go to school and get my education. I am very thankful to her for trusting in me and giving me a chance to experience a much better life than what I had living in Louisiana. I went on to obtain a bachelor's degree and master's degree, which I used to secure a thirty-plus-year career in health information management. It was a leap of faith to leave everything I had ever known to seek a better life, but one thing that I have always known about such life decisions is that you always want to move on to something better. You always want to progress and not regress!

My move up north was the start of my successful journey from poverty to prosperity. Sometimes you must move away from that which is familiar to move up in life. There were many more lessons that I learned along my road to success. *9 Steps from Poverty to Prosperity* will define the principles of navigating the road to success. I am sharing these lessons with you so that you, too, can move on from poverty to prosperity. Each chapter will define one of the principles of navigating the road to success, drawn from my own experiences to prove to you how true these principles are.

After reading this book I hope you:

- Will be inspired to take control of your own road to success and use the tools and principles I suggest.
- Be encouraged by my story that it is never too late to achieve your goals.
- Learn from my story that all obstacles can be overcome.

~ Notes for Discussion Questions ~

~ Notes for Discussion Questions ~

1

Overcoming a Poverty Mindset

Once I got an education and earned some money, I still had to get rid of my poverty mindset. I was always eager to spend my money on material things. There I was sitting in church one Sunday in the early '90s, and the minister was speaking about kindness. There were more than 3,000 people in our mega church, but it seemed as if the minister was speaking directly to me. He said, "Be careful how you treat others, and especially those that may be less fortunate, because a lot of people are just one paycheck away from being homeless. Let the church say, amen."

The minister may have been talking about kindness, but he called out my poverty mindset. Fear came over me as I realized I was just one paycheck away from disaster myself. I thought I could be homeless one day. Here I was in my early thirties, sitting in church, dressed up and broke. I needed help.

Up until that point, poverty to me simply meant not having enough money for my basic needs. I like to call it "being on the system." I always remembered getting free lunches at school or qualifying for a summer job because my family met the low-income guidelines.

Now I was an adult and had money to meet my basic needs but did not have any savings. I had no emergency fund and had acquired a lot of credit card debt. I had more than twenty credit cards; a few of them were maxed out and I was only paying the minimum amount due each month. I never read the fine print on the credit card bill that explained paying only the minimum amount each month would mean you could be paying off the debt for many, many years.

I could pay my bills and drive a new car but had no real savings account. A poverty mindset to me is also being fake. I was trying to look like and act like I had money when I was really living paycheck to paycheck, as the minister said. I used to hear my mom use the phrase, "Robbing Peter to pay Paul."

As a child, I realized that meant that you were still broke and lacking, and in other words Peter was not getting paid. I made sure the rent was paid and the car note was paid, but it seemed as if I wasn't getting paid enough, even though I was sometimes working three jobs at once. I have now learned it really does not matter how much money you have; you need to know how to manage it. I can now see how many people can go from having millions to being homeless.

I knew I had to transform the way I viewed money. I started educating myself on debt and finances. I started reading books on being debt free and I attended seminars on financial literacy. At a singles conference put on by my church, I submitted the question, "What does it mean to be debt free?" but I did not really think it would be answered. However, the facilitator selected the question. "You cannot spend more than you earn, and no more than 30 percent of your money should be going toward a mortgage and car payment, and you should also pay yourself by setting something aside for an emergency."

At that time, I thought it would be a long time before I would be debt free. I was thinking, "You will always have some kind of debt."

I used to use about 50 percent of my earnings toward paying for my rent and car. I had no real savings and no emergency funds. I would occasionally do cash advances on a credit card, which I realize now is a much higher interest rate than on your credit card purchases.

There are many definitions of a poverty mindset. My own definition of it is to think short term and not long term, or to think of lack and not of abundance or tangible and not intangible. Getting rid of a poverty mindset is an ongoing process. You must take baby steps when you are learning a new skill like this. For my baby steps, I started paying out the smaller credit card bills first, and then the ones that I only opened to get a discount or a gift. There are instances when you open a credit card, you will get 20 percent off of your first purchase, which usually includes the sale price. Some of the department stores will not let you pay the card off right away; they will give you a temporary card that is good for one day. You will get the credit card later and if you are not disciplined, you will continue to use it. You must be aware of the mark-ups and other tactics that are being used by some of the stores. Many of these discounts may not be worth pursuing. I had a credit card that I never used which was from a jewelry store. I am so glad that diamonds were never my best friend. It took me several years to pay off most of the credit cards. I was using those credit cards as security, but I realized that it was not very smart to have that many credit cards. Now, I only have a few credit cards that I use occasionally.

I have now taken the advice of a former colleague to pay my credit cards off completely when I get the bill to avoid that interest accruing each month. In the past, I couldn't see that at the time because I had so many outstanding balances. I consistently follow this advice now that I have obtained financial literacy. As the saying goes, when you know better you do better. In the past, when I was approved for a credit card, I thought that was financial freedom and I had arrived. I went to some seminars on debt that suggested that you cut up your credit cards, freeze them (literally submerge them in water and put them in the freezer), or leave them at home when going shopping, but none of that helped me because of my poverty mindset. If I left my credit cards at home, I would just show my driver's license and still use them. Today, I do not make purchases unless I know I will pay them off at the end of the month. I have been delivered from that impulse buying. There will always be another sale!

Early on in my quest to become debt-free, I realized that I had a long way to go, but I felt that one day I would eventually get out of debt and make my money work for me and not everyone else. And that positive approach served me well. I wish I had learned earlier in my life about managing finances and debt. I appreciate all the people that helped me along the way. One way to get rid of a problem is to seek help or learn about the problem and what is causing it. I learned about debt and therefore was able to become debt free. It did not happen overnight, but it did happen. Believe in yourself and know that you can have what you want to achieve if you work hard at it.

My husband is from a family of seven. He told me how his father taught him about money at an early age. He worked in a liquor store a block away from his house when he was only ten-years-old. He was paid one dollar a week to clean up around the store and sweep the inside of the store. He said that the owner asked if he wanted a box of candy or one dollar a week as pay. He said that he wanted the money. My husband later explained to me that the candy was material, and he decided on the money. When he first told me the story, I looked at it the wrong way and wondered why his parents would let him work at a liquor store as a child. Of course, times have changed, and he said he was able to do that back then. He later told me how he would put the money in a little bank and save it until he had enough money to buy a coat. It was the difference in how we were brought up. My husband said they did not always have a lot, but his father always taught him about finances. The difference between my husband and myself is that I only knew lack as a child, so when I finished college and obtained some money, I focused on material things. I have now learned it really does not matter how much money you have; you need to know how to manage it. Having a poverty mindset from childhood prevents many people from knowing how to manage their money.

My Aunt Gladys always tells me that she knows how to manage money. She bought a house when she was in her late forties and always had a new car. She always had a savings account. I usually send her money for Christmas and other times throughout the year. My aunt will often tell me that she still has not spent the money I sent her, and she will usually say that she is saving it to purchase something that she needs. I know the younger version of me would never do that. My mom would tell me when I had some money as a kid that the money was burning a hole in my pocket, which meant that I wanted to go to the store and spend it quickly, usually for snacks. I would never have saved it. Again, I had to overcome that poverty mindset and lack mentality.

All that debt that I had incurred was due to impulse buying. I am now able to be more aware of my urges toward impulsivity. One motto that I like to be guided by is, "I control my money, not everyone else!"

I have now moved beyond that poverty mindset. I invest in myself now, and money is no longer burning a hole in my pocket. I now have a better understanding of finances.

It's not how much money you have but it is knowing how to save it. One Bible verse that comes to mind is Proverbs 4:7, which states, "Wisdom is the principal thing; therefore, get wisdom. And with all thy wisdom get understanding."

We have all heard of athletes and entertainers who became millionaires and later became broke. If you have money, you still need to understand how to use it wisely. You need to acquire wisdom to manage your money, or any other challenges and obstacles that you face, that could cause you to lose everything you have worked so hard for.

Discussion Questions

1. What is a poverty mindset?

2. Have you ever thought that you would be homeless?

3. Can you name some ways people may become homeless?

4. Do you think financial literacy should be taught in high school?

~ Notes for Discussion Questions ~

~ Notes for Discussion Questions ~

2

Finding Positive Role Models

It is good to have positive role models. A role model could be a friend, celebrity, relative, or anyone that you would like to pattern your life after in some aspect. The first step to moving on to a more successful life is to have a positive role model. My aunt was someone who I saw as a role model when I moved from Louisiana to Michigan as a teenager. She was someone who I would look up to when she would come to visit us in Louisiana. She would buy us some clothes and help us financially.

When I moved on to seek a better life in Detroit, I tried to hang around positive people or people who wanted something out of life. These were people that would always try and encourage me, even when I sometimes wanted to give up. I recall one Sunday school teacher I had that would always build us up and tell us to try to stay positive and move on even if we made mistakes. It takes more energy to tear someone down, and you should look for someone to build you up and believe in you. You must also believe in yourself.

I grew up going to a Baptist church when I was a child. When I moved to Detroit, I went to the Pentecostal church that my aunt attended. It was a different kind of church for me and a unique experience. The church had about 250 members, so that seemed like a large church to me at that time. It had a lot of older members and a few people that were my age. These church members were lively and did a lot of upbeat singing and shouting. It was what I thought in my mind at that time as a "fire and brimstone" church. After I was able to afford a car, I moved on to a non-denominational church that I chose myself and that really changed my life. My pastor not only preached about Godly living but also taught us about relationships, serving, being faithful, getting out of debt, and obtaining wealth, among other topics. My understanding of church when I was growing up was usually a "come to Jesus" talk every Sunday, or a message that you must love everybody. I was so excited about my new church—I learned the scriptures about wealth, serving others, and other biblical quotes that helped me to stay strong and never give up. That was the beginning of changing my mindset from poverty to prosperity. It was when I discovered my passion in life to help others, because I realized there were those that God had placed in my family life to help us; agencies such as the Doll and Toy Fund and a grocery store that let my mom have food on credit so that we would not have to go hungry. I had a revelation that I would be rich one day, and wanted to pay back the kindness I had received in my youth to one day be a blessing to others.

Webster's Dictionary gives one definition of rich as "abundant." We had a lack of money when I was growing up, but I knew that would one day change. I did not know when, but I had that image firmly planted in my mind. The pastor at my chosen church became my role model. He talked about how he had moved on from a denominational church to a non-denominational church.

If you want to succeed in life, look at people who are successful and can have a positive influence on your life. I started going to seminars and learning about debt and money long before I started on my journey from poverty to prosperity. I did not want to be around people that were always talking about not having money and saying that no one could ever get ahead in life. I wanted to hear from people that believed that anyone could have a better life than they had if they worked hard at it. You must believe you can do better. It does not matter if others believe in you. You must believe in yourself!

What Happens if you do not have Positive Role Models?

If you do not have positive role models, you may have to learn the hard way about some things in life. I did not have any positive role models growing up that I could pattern my career after. I always desired to be a lawyer. I did not have the career counseling opportunities that are available today. I did have some colleagues that always gave me good advice later in life. Once I took some career assessments in college, I always did very well in the legal aspects of the tests. I was always one that tried to learn from others in life; people that continue to encourage me today. I always talk to my aunt, and she tells me how hard she had to work due to her lack of education. That always helps me to want to finish strong in whatever I start in life. I continue to be a lifelong learner. If you do not have positive role models, I still think that you can succeed in life. You should always pattern your life on what you want to do and not what someone else want you to do.

What Happens if Your Role Models are Negative?

I once knew someone who had a son that was an honor roll student. The young man got in some trouble after hanging out with the wrong crowd and spent some time in a penal institution. The role model that was mentoring him became ill and died. He no longer had a positive role model to look up to. I think we should always have someone we look up to that inspires us. There were colleagues of mine that always encouraged me when I was working part time while attending college. Some of the employees told me that it took them years to finish college, but they still finished.

Society seems to want to define what a role model is today. You can be the best version of yourself. I recall that when I was in management some of my co-workers would tell me that I should dress for my future career. I did not really understand what they meant at that time. I think if you want to have a good role model, you need to look at how that person cares for themselves. Look at how they talk and not at what they do and how much money they make. If you hang around people that are negative all the time, that attitude will rub off on you. Just because people have made a mistake in life does not disqualify them from being role models. They can always serve as a cautionary tale to discourage people from not doing as they did.

Qualities of a Role Model

Do not put role models on a pedestal. We are all human and make mistakes. Do not think that role models have to be perfect. The qualities I would look for in a role model are that they are someone who listens, someone who helps their community, and someone that cares about people. Look at a role model as being a road map to your future; someone that can guide you in life. This person may be a teacher, pastor, friend, actor, sports figure, or someone else.

Becoming a Role Model

I had a friend who lived with his grandmother until he was twelve-years-old, and then he went to live with his mom. He did not have a relationship with his dad. My friend told me that he was angry growing up and decided to join a junior gang. He eventually went to prison for ninety-days. He later told me the story of how prison changed his life. He may not have known what he wanted to do, but he did know what he did not want to do, and that was to be a career criminal. He spent his three months there surrounded by fights. He said that when his ninety-days were up, he looked the correctional officer in the eye when he was leaving and said, "You'll never see me again!"

My friend said, that was almost fifty years ago, and he grew up to have a family and a successful career. He realized that a life of crime was not for him. He was a skilled tradesman and would often speak on career day at some of the local colleges. I would say he became his own role model when he took control of his life by not letting his past determine his future.

We can all be role models in life. When I was an adjunct instructor, I would always tell the students how to conduct themselves during their internships. My professors told me the same thing about my own internship. People are watching you and you always want to make a good impression, especially when you are trying to succeed in your career. I always reminded them to be professional, be on time, and be courteous to those that were helping them. I would also give them a heads up if I heard any negative information in general about other students on an internship. My department head once told me about a student that was not dressed professionally on an internship site. I reminded the students without going into too much detail the importance of appropriate attire. The inappropriately dressed intern was not a student from the location where I taught, but it was a good, gentle reminder to them. I still had a couple of students that stayed connected with me after I stopped teaching. I have been a role model to a lot of my students. I wanted to be their teacher and one thing I wanted them to be was successful.

Discussion Questions

1. What would you look for in a role model?

2. Who do you think of as a good role model?

3. Would you like to be a role model?

4. What traits do you need to be a good role model?

5. What can a role model learn from you?

6. Did you have any role models growing up?

7. Who were your role models growing up?

8. Can a fictitious character be a role model?

3

Get Educated

One way to overcome poverty is to get educated. Getting educated does not necessarily mean getting a college degree. There are many trades and skill sets that can be acquired that can help a person earn a decent wage to take care of themselves and a family that does not require a college degree. A great example is my former repair person, 1 will call him Alfred. Alfred told me that he did not finish high school. Alfred later obtained a general educational development (GED) and earned more than some college graduates as a carpenter. Education does not have to come from books but can also be gained from life experiences. However, there are many benefits to getting a formal education.

Having an education can provide you with better career advancement opportunities. I have a bachelor's degree in health services administration with several certifications in medical coding and health information management. I have had several jobs in the health care field that allowed me to work in the insurance industry, educational institutions, as well as for the federal government. Several jobs have certain educational requirements just to get an interview, and some have other preferences. Several years ago, certain jobs would ask for a medical coding certificate, but over the years medical coding became more specialized and advanced and a basic certification would not get your foot in the door. The world is constantly changing, so the more we advance our education the better career advancement opportunities will be available. I was laid off once for about two months, and during some of that time I was taking a small break, but the rest of the time I spent deciding which job to accept. Having a college degree can increase your chances of being employed.

Having an education gives you a better chance of earning more money. I once worked at a job where there were people that had been at the company for years, but certain job postings would sometimes have bachelor's or master's degree required. So, if you have a plethora of experience in an area, having a degree could make you more marketable. One way to increase your chances for career advancement and more money is to invest in your education. When I was at a dead-end in my career at one time, I invested in obtaining my master's degree. I was able to obtain a position as an adjunct professional and taught allied health courses at Davenport University in Dearborn and Livonia, Michigan.

Being educated can also help you develop your circle of professional networks. I joined some professional networks as a student, and there were always individuals present at some of the professional organizations that had job postings and sometimes were looking for students or other individuals to fill a position. I would always encourage my students to join some of the organizations in their perspective fields. I was hired because one of my colleagues told me about a position and said it was okay to tell the employer that they had referred me. I have also received a nice referral bonus for referring someone else for a job. There are other benefits of networking, such as keeping abreast of the latest things that are going on in your field. You can also network by applying for certain professional magazines that list postings for jobs. I have also been hired from applying for positions that were listed in a professional journal. Networking can be important in your journey to success. Look at it as meeting different people from diverse backgrounds and skill sets.

Getting an education can allow you to have better health benefits and a healthier lifestyle as well. I remember as a child I had to go to the charity hospital when I was sick, which was a hospital for low-income people and those without health insurance. We would have to get a ride with a relative or call a cab to go to this hospital. It usually was a long wait of a few hours to be seen by a doctor. As a child, I do not remember my family ever having health insurance. I had poor eyesight as a child because my parents could not afford to buy me eyeglasses. I remember being in the eighth grade and my teacher asked me to read a question from the board and answer it. My classmate sitting next to me knew that I could not see the board and quietly read the question to me. I repeated it and was able to answer it correctly. I now realize the importance of having health benefits and am now able to correct some of the problems that I could not when I was living in poverty, such as getting my eyes and teeth checked annually.

I got a summer job when I was about fourteen-years-old through a low-income program that allowed those eligible to work for eight weeks. I bought my first pair of glasses, and the lenses were very thick. I would put them on in school if I had to read something on the board. My classmates would tease me because of the thick lenses, so I was embarrassed to wear them on a regular basis. I would squint my eyes to try and see the blackboard without the glasses. Fast forward to today, I thank God for technology because I now have multi-focal eyeglasses and contact lenses, so no one knows that I am very near-sighted except for me and my eye doctor. I am so grateful now to have health insurance that allows me to go to the appropriate physicians when needed to help me live a healthier lifestyle.

Having a degree can allow you to work in a certain field. If you want to be a physician, you have several specialties to choose from. The same is true for a teacher or lawyer. It could allow you to further pursue your passion, and allows you to be more diverse, which could lead to higher income for some specialties.

Being educated can help you to obtain overall knowledge about life circumstances and the world system and how it works. I once worked at a job where my supervisor gave me a write up for a no call, no show. I challenged it through the human resources department, and it was reversed and taken out of my file. I had called my supervisor on the day of the incident and told her that my car had broken down and that if I could get it fixed that it was a possibility that I might still be able to make it to work, but if not, I was not going to be in that evening. This position was a part-time evening position at which I was working a four-hour shift. My supervisor was ending her shift when I started mine, so we would see each other for about a half hour before she left. I never had any issues with the supervisor; the position was flexible, and I was always able to adjust my hours if needed. The write-up was somewhat of a surprise. I had been in management before, so

I knew that I was within my rights to challenge my supervisor's decision. I had contacted my supervisor that day and she knew or should have known that there was a possibility that I would not be able to get my car fixed, therefore, I would not have been able to make it to work. I could have easily let it go, but because I was educated on employment-related matters, I knew that this was something that I had to address.

Being educated can allow you to broaden your horizons. Sometimes society wants everyone to think alike, but it is okay to agree to disagree. I remember years ago there were some people with a petition that had language on it that was misleading. These people were standing outside of grocery stores asking customers if they wanted to sign the petition. I do not sign my name on anything if I do not know what it is. My husband always tells me that I think "Mr. Google" knows everything. If I do a google search on something, I am going to do further research through other sources. When I lived in Detroit, at one time there were a lot of houses in foreclosure. Just like there were reports of an increase in fraud during the pandemic, there were those in the housing industry trying to take advantage of people trying to buy homes. I once had someone warn me that people were saying that if you bought a foreclosed house, they would give you a house free. It was so funny to me, but I was wondering who would fall for that. One idiom that I always heard growing up was not to take any wooden nickels. I am not saying that I have not fallen for some trickery, but the more educated you are about what is going on, the less your chance of being fooled.

The benefits of an education, whether it's a college degree or skilled trade training, can increase your chance of better employment; you can get a job in almost any industry and make a living more than if you did not have any skill sets at all. It also allows you to be independent. When you live in poverty, you may have to live in a certain neighborhood or go to a certain school. The opposite is true when you have a higher income. You can live in a certain neighborhood and go to a certain school if you have the money to pay for it. When I was a child, when my family was on government assistance, we could get things based on my family's income. I didn't learn how to drive until I was in my twenties, but there were students I went to high school with whose families could afford for them to take driver's education, and some of them had their own cars. I am not saying that your education will cause you to be a millionaire, but it can open many doors when you have a college degree or a skilled trade.

One additional benefit of being educated is that those who want a better life do not have to be involved in criminal activity. I have heard that people that are incarcerated will continue to commit crimes if they are unable to get a job when they leave prison. There are some prisons that allow inmates to start skilled trades in prison such as culinary arts, body shop mechanics, or other trades. It starts with educating your mind. I know of people who have entered the penal system and did not make a career out of it. I always try to encourage people and tell them to not to let society define them. You decide what you want to do and who you want to be.

Discussion Questions

1. How has being educated helped your career?

2. Do you think you would be making more money if you were not educated?

3. If you could change anything about your career, what would it be?

4. Are you satisfied with your career?

5. If you could go back to college, would you choose a different career?

6. What do you see as the biggest thing holding you back in your career?

7. What are you passionate about in life?

8. What would be your dream job?

9. Have you pursued all your dreams?

10. What would you like to see yourself doing in the next five years?

~ Notes for Discussion Questions ~

4

It is Never Too Late to Have Dreams Come True

What is it that you want out of life? It is never too late to pursue what you want. Is it a new job, a personal relationship, to learn a new skill, or something else? I am always amazed when I see people do something that society said they could not do, or that they thought was impossible. It all starts with changing your mindset.

Everyone has heard of "The American Dream," but it may mean different things to different people. One thing that it means to me is to go after the things that you desire and believe that you can have them if you do not give up.

It's Never Too Late for Friends

Most of us would say that we have friends, but some people may not have a lot of friends. To have friends, we must first want to have them. Define what type of friends you want. Do you want loyal friends? Friends that have your best interest at heart. Friends that will look out for you.

Everyone is not your friend! Our parents may have told us when we were kids to not call everyone your friend, especially if you did not know them. The same should apply when you are an adult. You never will know everything about everyone, but I would say that you should have some things in common as a basis for friendship, particularly in our busy adult lives.

I moved back to Louisiana after living in Michigan for thirty years, and I had to meet new friends at work and at church. I chose people with whom I had something in common to get to know better and had to learn how to be a friend to all these people. I still have my friends out of state. Some have come to visit me, and the others stay connected by email, telephone, or via text.

You get to choose your friends, and it is okay if someone does not want to be your friend. It is a personal choice, and each individual gets to decide who they let into their life. We all live busy lives, but we still must put in the time when we want to invest in a good friendship. It is a clever idea to take an inventory of your friends occasionally and see if they are worth pursuing; no one wants friends that never call you or check on you or friends that only call when they want something. These are usually fair-weather friends or users. I usually put them on the do not call or block list.

It is never too late to meet new friends. I have friends that are in my age group, older friends, and younger friends, and I have learned so much from each of them. Good friends should not be afraid to tell you when you are wrong. They should be there for you in the good times and the bad times, and they should always try to build you up and not tear your down. This works both ways. My suggestion to anyone that wants to have friends is to be friendly, cherish any good friends you have, and practice the golden rule of trying to be the type of friend that you would want others to be to you.

It is Never Too Late for a New Career

Are you tired of your job? You don't have to keep it. You can transition into a new career. What is it that you like to do? Do you like helping people? Do you like working with a group as part of a team or alone? I always like to encourage people to go after what they want in life. I decided to pursue my passion as a motivational speaker after I spent over thirty years working in health care.

It Is Never Too Late for Close Partner Relationships

I have always desired a mate. I moved back home to Louisiana after almost thirty years in Michigan when I was fifty-years-old. I moved to another part of Louisiana from the small city that I grew up in. After attending a church in my new city, I decided to explore other areas of the state to worship. I googled a couple of churches that were about twenty-five miles from where I lived. I must say I have no sense of direction when it comes to traveling and got lost when I was headed to one of the churches that I had planned to visit one Sunday. I never did find that church, however, instead of going back home I said to myself, "I will try church number two."

I almost did not find church number two because it was not visible from the street. Sometimes in life your dreams and goals may not seem to be near, but that is not to say that they are that far off. I finally found church number two and wrote the directions down much more clearly and went back home. The following Sunday, I went to church number two. I had missed my church in Michigan, and it is never a good idea to compare people or places with someone or something else. I did not want to be without a church home, so I decided to join the church. A lot of churches are eager to get members to volunteer, so when I was asked about joining an auxiliary, I decided on being an usher. I had been an usher at my previous church for six years.

Volunteering is not often given the recognition that it deserves. Volunteering is something that is freely done and has many inherent rewards. I would always get to church early because it was about a twenty-five-mile drive from my house. I would often see a nicely dressed man sitting in front of me with a couple that I later found out were his brother and sister-in-law. I said a polite hello to him one Sunday and he did not respond. I would describe myself as an introvert, and thought to myself, "He will not get a hello from me again."

Later, as I was talking to one of my usher friends, the non-responder passed by us and she greeted him, and he was jovial and responded. I told her about the incident when he did not respond to me. She replied that sometimes you must make sure that a person hears you. A few months later, this man inquired about me. I would sit on the church pew usually behind his brother and his wife, but I did not know that they were related to him at the time. The non-responder asked his brother what kind of person I was, and his brother told him that he really did not know me but his wife overhead the conversation and told him that I seemed like a nice person. The funny thing is that his brother thought he was talking about someone else with the same name. The non-responder later said he told his brother that he was asking about Sylvia "the usher."

A few months later, the non-responder joined the usher board, and we would have little friendly chats and I learned that his name was Johnny. Johnny and I would always chat in the parking lot because we got to church at the same time due to us both ushering. A few months later, he asked me if I wanted to go out to lunch, and we started doing that occasionally after church. We became good friends, and two years later he asked me to marry him, and I said yes! We just celebrated five years of marriage.

My friends and family were surprised because they knew I had a friend, but they did not know it was serious. I was the poster child for being single because I was a career-driven woman and did not do a lot of dating. I also realized early on in life that I had the gift of goodbye. I would not hang around people, jobs, or any other things that I felt were not for me. I always desired to be married but just did not shout it from the rooftops. I never wanted to be alone the rest of my life and knew I would eventually meet someone.

So, whatever you want in life, go for it! Don't let society dictate to you what you can and cannot have. You never know who and what will come across your path, be it the right person, right job, or something else. Do not make assumptions about people and situations that you do not know anything about. My husband later told me that he never even saw me or heard me speak to him because he does not have peripheral vision in one eye. He said I was on the side where he could not see me. He refers to it as his bad side. When he saw me on the usher board, I must have been on his "good" eye side. He decided to inquire about "Sylvia" the usher.

Discussion Questions

1. Why do people give up on their dreams or goals?

2. Why do people give up on themselves?

3. Do you think it is too late to achieve your dreams or goals?

4. Is fear the reason that you have not had success in pursuing your dreams or goals?

5. Have you ever accomplished something that you did not believe you could obtain?

5

Ask For Help

The Benefits of Asking for Help

It is okay to ask for help. One of the bible verses that I heard a lot
as a child was Matthew 7:7 which states, "Ask, and it shall be given
you; seek, and ye shall find; knock, and it shall be opened unto you."

I remember arriving in Detroit with little clothes, money, or
other necessities. I had a pair of glasses that were broken and
had only one handle. One of my contact lenses was torn. At that
time, I had replaceable contact lenses that cost $30 for one. I did
not have $30 dollars to replace the contact lens, so I just wore
one. I am extremely nearsighted, and I knew that was making my
vison worse. I finally told my aunt that one of my contact lenses
had torn and asked if she could give me the money to replace it,
which she did.

I look back at that today and realize how crazy it was for me to
do that. My aunt brought me into her home. I was too embarrassed
to tell her about the contact lens because I thought she would fuss
and/or complain. My aunt did not have a lot of money, but she was
always willing to share what she had with me. There is sometimes

shame that comes from asking for help; we sometimes have the fear of rejection or the fear of being told no. There are benefits to asking for help. We have all needed or will need help at one point in our lives. I was able to see better when I was able to get the money to replace the torn contact lens. I had just learned to use the public transportation system in Detroit, and I needed to be able to see the bus signs and street signs so I could know that I was going in the right direction. There is nothing worse than being in a new city and looking lost. By asking for help, I gave myself confidence and lessened the anxiety of not being able to see clearly, and of course it helped me to get on the right bus to get to my destination.

When I first enrolled in college, I did not have any money to pay for the first semester because my student loan had not yet been finalized. I told my aunt that I needed about $300 to enroll for the first semester. My aunt asked one of her church members to loan her the money and told her that we would pay her back later, which I did as soon as possible.

I have asked for help several times when I genuinely needed it. When I first started Mercy College of Detroit, I took eighteen credits the first semester, which was five classes. I was failing one of the classes and had to withdraw from it. My academic advisor told me that would delay my graduation for the associate degree that I was going to pursue initially so that I could get a job while I continued working toward my bachelor's degree. I was working part-time at a local hospital and while talking with one of my coworkers I told her that I was going to be delayed in getting my associates degree. The small liberal arts college that I was attending offered most classes just once a year. My co-worker told me about a community college that was offering a similar class the following semester that was equivalent to the class that I was failing. By discussing the class with my co-worker, I learned some useful information. I graduated on time with my associate degree in the Medical Records Science Program. If I had not asked for help, I would have had to delay my education. Don't be ashamed to ask for help; everyone may need help at one point in life.

When People Say No

If you ask and don't get the answer that you want, that's okay! As the saying goes, "No can just mean not now." I contacted the executive director of a local charitable organization that I supported about giving a free speech to their group but was told that because of the pandemic I could not come in person or do it virtually. A couple of months later, the same director called and emailed me to ask me if I would give them permission to be quoted in an article that she had asked me to write about how I was supporting the organization financially. I did not get to speak at the organization, but I was given an opportunity to write an article regarding the importance of giving to charities on a regular basis.

When people say no, they sometimes are doing you a favor. I look back at all the times that I have been told no in my life and I think that a lot of them were blessings in disguise. If I had not been denied many job requests in my previous career in healthcare, I may still be in that industry and not pursuing my passion in life. So, when people say no, know that they have the right to say no, just like there are times when we have to say no in life.

Learning Lessons from Hearing No

I had a friend for about ten years, and once we both moved out of state, we lost contact with each other. I tried a telephone number I had, then an email address, and was finally able to connect with her by text. I asked her if we could chat and catch up on what was going on in our lives. We had both always cherished each other's friendship. I remembered our laughs together and just the fun times that I had with her and her family. She always sought my advice, and I would seek advice from her, as well. My ex-friend responded to the text and said that her number had been the same for all those years. She did not respond to the text after that. I took that as a no to rekindling our friendship. I gave her the "gift of goodbye." She did not want to be bothered by me and that was no problem. We must respect people's wishes when they do not want to be bothered. I usually have a simple remedy for that; it's called "block the number." I do not want to accidentally dial or text that person by mistake.

My husband shared with me that when he first moved back to Louisiana, he called up a friend to tell him that he was back in town. The friend wanted to know how long he had been back in town, and he told him a couple of months. His friend responded, "You have been back that long and are just now calling me?"

He did talk to him, but my husband said the friend never called back. He said that he sees him occasionally, but they do not stay connected. He said that they went to school together and used to be good friends. Unlike me, my husband said that he would talk to him if he called, but I cut off relationships unless both agreed to be friends. My mother used to tell me when I was younger to not "run" behind someone that seemed like they did not want to be bothered. I like people to appreciate my friendship, so now I am careful to whom I give my energy. If you are calling all the time and checking in on people that do not want to be bothered, then it is time to let them go. You do not choose your family, but you do choose your friends.

There is Power in Saying No

How many times have we said yes to something that we should have said no to? No gives you the power to set boundaries and to be yourself. We always feel that we should give an explanation to people when we say no, but we are not required to do so. Learn to live life on your own terms and not on everyone else's. Do what makes you happy and continue to pursue your passion in life!

Risks of Asking for Help and How to Manage It

There I was, driving in Michigan on a snowy road in February and it was getting dark. I had moved out of Michigan about two years prior and had returned to visit for a surprise birthday party for my aunt. I was in a small rental car and was trying to be extremely cautious due to not having driven in snow in a while. I was looking for the hotel I was staying in. I must say that I am very "directionally challenged."

I checked into the hotel and went to visit some friends in Detroit. The GPS kept telling me to make a right turn, but I did not see the hotel anywhere in sight. I did not want to call my aunt because she did not know that I was in town. I began to panic; it was in the winter and almost nighttime. I saw some people coming from one of the large corporate buildings in the area and drove up to the entrance where the cars were exiting the parking lot. I rolled down my window and stopped and began to politely ask a guy if he knew where the hotel that I was looking for was. He did not want to have anything to do with me. He shooed me away and said "no, no," as if to say, "Get away from me lady!"

I drove away; however, I did not give up. I circled the parking lot and saw a lady walking out of the parking lot, I politely rolled down the window again and told the lady that I was lost and asked her if she knew where the hotel that I was looking for was. She pointed about a half block away and said to make a "quick" right when I got to one of the fast-food restaurants. She looked a little hesitant, but she did help me, and I felt bad because I was not too far from the hotel.

I understand that in the times we live in, it is hard to trust anyone. I got to the hotel and the next day, I went to the restaurant and met some of my aunt's church members, and of course she was glad to see me. When I returned home, it came to me about the gentlemen that shooed me away that he may have thought that I was an undercover police officer. I started to laugh so hard, but I realized that he was being wise. I would have had the same reaction if a person had approached me asking about a hotel.

When I lived in Michigan and would visit my family in Louisiana, one of my relatives would tease me because I always carried a purse. I was told that some of the people in the area may have thought that I was an undercover police officer, because no one walked around that area with a purse.

They said that I needed to update my style and carry a backpack.

There are risks in asking for help because you are vulnerable. I was letting the people know that I was lost and was not familiar with the area. I did not get out of the car, but I was putting myself in some danger. There are some risks in asking for help, but do not let that deter you from asking; you must have courage and ask for help when needed. The hotel was sitting off the street and with no straightforward signs. I had wasted about twenty minutes looking for the hotel on my own, but I was glad the second person that I asked for help took the time to give me better directions to the hotel.

I will share with you one other time that I asked for help and realized that it was a risk accepting it. I was in a car accident years ago, and the car dealership had a backlog of cars and told me that it could be three to four weeks before they could fix my car. My insurance company told me that I could take it somewhere else, and they would still pay for it. I asked a few people if they could recommend someone. The person that I ended up talking to about my car stated that the place that he was referring me to would waive my deductible, but if anything happened that was between me and his friend. I did not like the sound of that. I ended up taking my car to the dealership and it did take a month to complete, but at least I had dealt with that car dealership before and never had any issues with them in repairing my car. The one that stated his friend would waive the $500 deductible may have been reputable, but it may have taken longer than a month to complete. I was aware of a potential risk, so I did not let them fix my car. I recalled that one of my colleagues had someone fix her car and it took them over three months to get it fixed. She had to get a ride to work because she could not afford to keep the rental car for that length of time. That was the first thing that came to my mind when the guy told me that his friend would waive my $500 deductible to fix my car, but how long would I have had to wait to get the car back? I find it is important to listen to your instincts. If you heart tells you "go forward," more often than not you will be fine.

Why is it Hard to Ask for Help?

Why is it hard for people to ask for help? They may worry that they will be rejected or may feel embarrassed. It's okay to ask for help. To move on in life, there will come a time that you will need help. Whenever I was seeking employment, I would look online for career opportunities and ask some of my previous co-workers about some job leads. I have also helped some of my colleagues with obtaining employment. I was once given a $500 bonus for referring a former co-worker to a company where I used to work. I encourage you to continue to keep on your journey of success; you never know how and when you will be rewarded.

People are afraid to ask for help sometimes because of their fear of rejection. I had an older friend that did not know how to drive, so I would pick her up and sometimes would run errands for her. She lived in the same area that I did so it was not a problem. A few times she told me that she was hesitant to call me because she knew that I had a busy schedule at that time and she did not want to bother me. I told her to always call me ahead of time if possible and I would let her know if I could do it. It worked out for both of us most of the time. I was in her shoes at one time, and I did not want to ask anyone for help. We went to the same church and lived close to each other. I was not going out of my way to help her. She later moved further away, and she was considerate and did not ask me to take her places after she moved, especially if it was at night. I have in the past taken people home that lived some distance away. It was okay occasionally, but I did not like going so far out of my way. I would just let that person know that I could not take them home anymore.

Sometimes people are afraid of creating an obligation when asking for help. One of my colleagues would always invite me over to her house during the Super Bowl. I never went because I did want to feel obligated to go over to her house. We worked together for years and were friends, but I just did not ever want to go to her house. She would joke about it all the time. It was about a forty-five-minute drive, and she would say that most people went home at half time. I enjoyed her friendship, but I was not interested in visiting her every year for the Super Bowl.

I grew up learning from my family that you should try not to ask anyone for anything. My mentality was to not ask anyone for anything unless it was absolutely necessary. That is the wrong way to be. We live in a society where we may need someone to help us, whether it's for directions, a job, or anything else. I remember accepting a job one time and the lady that I thought I would be working with had quit the job before I accepted the position. I ended up working with someone that had a different management style than mine. That job ended up not working out for me. I later ran into the person that recommended me for the job and she apologized to me about the situation. I learned a lesson from not asking more questions before I accepted a job offer. The people that knew me later told me that they thought I knew of all the things that were going on at that company at the time and were surprised that I accepted the job.

Another reason some people find it hard to ask for help is there is sometimes a negative stigma around asking for help. I know some people that think that someone may not need help due to the type of car that they drive. I have known people that work at food distribution centers, and some would make comments that a lot of people came to get food that were in nice cars. Those people could have been picking up food for someone else that did not have a car. The person could have lost their job; you never know what the situation could have been. However, there are people in the world that think it is their job to judge other people. I can see why people do not ask for help, whether it's for financial, mental, or substance abuse help, or something else. Don't let people opinion stop you from getting the help you need.

Discussion Questions

1. What are some benefits of asking for help?

2. What are some benefits of helping others?

3. What are some things that you have said no to and regretted it?

4. Is "No" a bad word?

5. How has the word "No" empowered you?

6. What are some risks of asking for help?

7. Is it hard for you to ask for help?

8. From whom should you ask for help?

9. Is asking for help bad?

Notes for Discussion Questions

6

Know When to Move On

One way to know when it is time to move on is when you have come to a crossroads or dead-end in life. Merriam-Webster defines a crossroad as a place where two or more roads meet and a dead-end is a road that has no end or course of action that leads to nothing further. Did I hear a "Been there, done that?"

Not too long ago, I realized that my job had become stagnant, and I knew it was time to move on. I had been working remotely for the past ten years, and I would dread getting up in the morning to start work. I began to feel sick just thinking about the job and complained about it to anyone who would listen to me. I talked about quitting but was still trying to hold on because of the benefits. My husband got tired of me talking about the job and he said, "You need to quit talking about that job and just quit!"

I think he had become a prophet and didn't know it. After he said that, I could not wait for the weekend to be over so I could submit my resignation. I submitted my resignation and had planned to give two weeks' notice, but I got an unexpected bonus when my supervisor told me that was not necessary, but they would pay me for the next two weeks even though I did not need to return. That was in March 2022, and I have been happily unemployed since then.

I had been in the health field for over thirty years, and it was time to say goodbye to that chapter of my life. I did not do a grand gesture for my resignation. I just had a great revelation. It was time to say goodbye to the health care industry.

Think about what happens in life when you are at a physical crossroads or a dead-end street. You must decide what your next move is because there is no other way to go but to turn around. No one could make that decision to leave that job but me. I stepped out on faith and things have worked out fine. You must believe in yourself and not doubt when you want something better in life.

I know there are some situations that are easier than others. I once had a friend that I will call Dodie. I considered her a friend, but it came to a point that I had to move on from her. She would always invite me over to be with her family on the holidays. She would prepare all types of food and she would ask me how I liked certain dishes. I must admit that some were dishes that I did not care for, but of course, I did not want to tell her that. She would say, "Please don't waste my food," so I would just take small portions, and then she complains that I did not like any of her meals..

Dodie was a widow, and she would always make comments like, "I would not want to be a young single woman at this time because it's simply too hard to meet someone." She seems to just put out negative vibes sometimes and I did not like being around her at times, so I slowly distanced myself from her.

She was an older woman, and I was much younger. I just one day stop visiting her when she would invite me to her home. She always complained that I would go home so early when I would visit her. I told her at that time that it was because I had to get up at 3:45 a.m. to be at work by 5 a.m. I would volunteer to work holidays, so I did not have to feel bad about declining an invitation to visit her. She later caught on and realized that I did not want to be bothered and she would always ask. "What did I do to you?" I said nothing to her, but to myself, I just thought this person was always so negative about things and it was time for me to move on from that friendship. Whenever she would see one of our mutual friends she would tell her, "I do not know what I did to Sylvia, she's acting different. I don't think she wants to be bothered with me."

I had already told my friend that she did not do anything to me. People are in your life for a reason and a season. I was always cordial to her, but I just decided to cut off our friendship. You can give yourself permission to discontinue relationships that are not healthy.

One way that you can know that it is time to move on is when you are serving something, but it is not serving you. Think about a job that you have been on for years, and you are just there for a paycheck or benefits. I have been there and done that!

A few years ago, there I was, sitting in a doctor's office. The physician examined my neck and said, "You have Hashimoto's." It's a good thing that I had heard of the term before, or I may have run out of the office screaming and crying. What could have been a devastating diagnosis turned out to be a blessing in disguise. I later had to have my thyroid removed. I was told due to its size, I needed to have it done as soon as possible because it had become symptomatic. I was also told that I would have to be on medication for the rest of my life. I was out on medical leave for about eight weeks before my physician cleared me to go back to work. I was working remotely at that time; however, I had not fully gotten my voice back. I realized that I was not able to do that type of work anymore, so I decided to not return to that position. It was at that moment that I decided to move on from that type of work. I submitted my resignation and did not return to my previous job. I realized that it was time for me to pursue a new career.

I had been trying to hold on to my comfort zone, but it was anything but comfortable. I was at a dead-end in my career. My decision was that it was time to pursue a new career. It was then that I decided to pursue a career as a motivational speaker and tell my story of how I got to where I am today.

We can sometimes turn our test into a testimony. If I had not been diagnosed with Hashimoto's, I would have tried to hold on to that job. Some of the fatigue and symptoms that I was having at the time were due to the thyroid disease, which was causing me to be tired all the time. Not only was I tired and fatigued physically, but also mentally. However, I am looking forward to my new career and have let the past go.

I have had four different jobs within the last two years. The last one I had, I quit after six weeks. I remember a phrase that I heard as a child, "Jumping out of the frying pan into the fire." That's what I kept doing. Even though I had made the decision to get out of the health care industry, I just kept going from one job to another in health care. I realized that I needed to move on to the next chapter of my life. I always wanted to be a motivational speaker, so what better time to pursue a new career. I had to see what was on the other side of moving on.

Moving on may not be as difficult as you may think. The supervisor who gave me those two weeks of pay when I resigned left the door open for me to come back if I would like. I returned all of my equipment, did the company survey, and let them know that it was nothing personal, but in summary it was just time for me to move on. I knew that for the past few years that I had a job and not a career. The great revelation allowed me to pursue my passion of becoming a motivational speaker.

There is nothing wrong with moving on in life. Learn to live life on your own terms. There are times when people would stay at a job, church, or home their entire life. There is nothing wrong with that if that is your desire. Look at moving on as moving up. What if you are not getting promoted in a job? You may decide to go and assist another church or even called to pastor a church. I do not think you need anyone else permission to pursue your dreams or something else that you are passionate about.

Discussion Questions

1. Why is it so hard for people to move on?

2. What are some benefits of moving on?

3. What are some benefits of not moving on?

4. Have you ever moved on from something and it was not as difficult as you thought?

5. Do you feel yourself having to explain to people about a choice you made? (i.e., leaving a job, church, or something else.)

6. Have you ever had regrets about moving on?

7. Were you happy when you moved on?

8. What was something good that happened to you when you moved on?

9. What would you say to others who are afraid to take a "leap of faith?"

~ Notes for Discussion Questions ~

∼ Notes for Discussion Questions ∼

How to Get Wealthy

Wealth may mean a lot of different things to each person. I grew up knowing that I was poor. I always wanted to be rich. I always knew that the opposite of poor is rich or wealthy. I never said I wanted to be wealthy. Meriam-Webster Dictionary defines wealthy as having wealth, very affluent, characterized as abundance, ample. A couple of words that are opposite of wealthy are disadvantaged and broke. I would say that I grew up in a "disadvantaged and broke" home. Wealth is not a dollar amount to me, but it means being comfortable and not living paycheck to paycheck. I now have a wealthy mindset. I desire to be wealthy so that I am able to help others that are poor or disadvantaged. I have a vision that I will one day be wealthy.

One way to get wealthy is to pay off your credit card debt. Credit card debt is not secure debt. It took me years to pay off my credit card debt. It hindered some of my personal growth because there were some things that I wanted to do but could not afford to do because of the consumer debt. I had big dreams growing up but did not have the guidance to help me pursue my dreams or find my passion in life. Once I realized that I was enthusiastic about helping others, I knew that I needed to have more than enough resources to do it effectively. I had poor financial literacy, which meant that I did not have money. I had thousands of dollars in credit card debt. I was trying to look like I had money when I did not.

I dreamed that I would have enough financial resources one day so that I could help others. Once I became financially literate, it helped me to reach one of my goals to help others. I knew that the reason I got to eat and have clothes and toys as a child was because someone helped my family.

Another way to get wealthy is to have a positive mindset and always be willing to help others. It is always good to donate your time, but organizations need both time and money. I recall an organization when I was growing up called The Doll and Toy Fund that would always set a goal for a certain amount of money to ensure every child in need would get a toy. I would watch the number go from $50 to over $5000, and at that time that was enough money for every child in the small city where I grew up to be able to receive a toy during Christmas. There are many other organizations that give clothes and food throughout the year to those in need. As you can see, being wealthy or having money has its advantages.

Financial Literacy

One way that I am learning to get wealthy is to continue to seek financial literacy. It has been a process for me. One thing that I learned is that I do not need to keep up with all the latest fashions, cars, and other material things. I once had the same car for ten years. I realized that society sometimes judges people by material things. I used to spend a great deal of time investing in material things. I am now interested in long term goals and making my money work for me. There is no such thing as a get rich quick scheme. Financial literacy is a lifelong learning process. I would encourage those who want to be wealthy to gain financial literacy.

I remember hearing misinterpreted sayings quoted as a child, such as "money is the root of all evil" or "rich people are evil." Deuteronomy 8:18 from the Bible says, "But thou shalt remember the Lord thy God: for it is he that giveth thee power to get wealth."

God blessed me with wealth so that I can be a blessing to others. Remember two of the definitions for wealth is "abundance" and "ample." One definition of charity is a gift of money, or its equivalent, given to the needy. I understand generational wealth and saving for a rainy day but I also heard one preacher say that he has never seen a U-Haul hooked up to a hearse. In other words, no matter how much money you have you can't take it with you.

Wisdom is Key

One final way to get wealthy and maintain wealth is to use wisdom with money. I understand that there is joy in giving, but make sure you have control of your money. You should know what's coming in and going out. Do not let anyone else control your money. You cannot give to everything and everybody. Do not fall for the spirit of trickery and manipulation of people. If you give out to everyone and you have nothing coming in, then you can become the one that will be in need. I am not suggesting frugality but wisdom. When and if you get wealthy, I suggest that you invest in yourself, people, and humanity. Remember those that are less fortunate than you.

Discussion Questions

1. How do you define wealth?

2. Is wealth a certain amount of money?

3. What is the purpose of wealth?

4. Name something you would do if you were wealthy?

5. Is being wealthy evil?

6. What do you think about wealthy people?

7. What is one reason to be wealthy?

8. Does being wealthy make you happy?

9. What is an advantage of being wealthy?

10. What is a disadvantage of being wealthy?

~ Notes for Discussion Questions ~

~ Notes for Discussion Questions ~

8

Be True to What You Know is Right

I once exposed government fraud and received a financial reward. Centers for Medicare and Medicaid Services (CMS) is part of the Department of Health and Human Services (HHS). CMS defines fraud as an intentional deception or misrepresentation with the knowledge that the deception could result in some unauthorized benefit to himself or some other person. Medicare fraud can happen anywhere, and usually it results in higher health care costs and taxes for everyone. Some examples include: a provider billing for services or supplies that the patient never received, a person using someone else's Medicare number or card to submit claims in their name, a provider charging Medicare twice for a service a patient only received once, or the anti-kick-back statute (AKS), etc. A person who reports fraud to the government is called a relator or whistleblower.

There can be risks involved in uncovering fraud, such as employee retaliation, discrimination, or career risks. Government fraud is not a victimless crime; it eventually affects all taxpayers. The government can decide to pursue or decline the case depending on the circumstances. They are usually not timely; they can take years to pursue. It does not matter but it is worth pursuing it when you are true to what is right and have your information together.

There are many fraud schemes today, and that was especially true during the pandemic. I spent over thirty years in the health field and know that there are lots of fraudulent billing schemes. The department of Health and Human Services Office of Inspector General, along with law enforcement partners, participated in the largest coordinated law enforcement action to combat health care fraud related to COVID-19. Fourteen defendants in seven federal districts across the United States were charged for their alleged participation in various health care fraud schemes that exploited the COVID-19 pandemic and resulted in over $1.2 billion in false billings. Defendants include telemedicine companies, executives, physicians, marketers, and medical business owners.

My experience in health care afforded me the opportunity to familiarize myself with what the Office of Inspector General (OIG) was targeting each year. I was aware of the various billing schemes. I started my career in coding and auditing and was a revenue audit contractor (RAC) auditor for years. The RAC was created through the Medicare Modernization Act of 2003 to identify and recover Medicare payments paid to health care providers under the fee for services (FFS) Medicare plans.

Qui Tam Relator

The False Claims Act (FCA) allows citizens to bring actions against companies and individuals for committing fraud against the government. I was one of those individuals. Under the FCA, the Qui Tam Relator will work with the government in prosecuting these cases in order to recover damages. To be a Qui Tam Relator, you must have some knowledge of the company or person committing the fraud. The Qui Tam provision was designed to encourage people to come forward so the money could be recovered from the fraud committed. The Qui Tam Relator is also protected from retaliation from the company or individuals committing the fraud. There are some factors that are necessary for a whistleblower to be eligible for a potential award. One of the elements is that only one person is eligible to file a reward for an allegation against a company. You must have good evidence and not just hearsay, and the fraud must have been committed against the federal government. Another element is that the company or person had knowingly committed fraud or intended to commit fraud.[1]

Whistleblower Rewards

According to the Justice Department, FCA settlements and judgments exceeded \$5.6 billion in Fiscal Year 2021.[2] The whistleblower can receive between 15-25 percent of the amount depending on how much is recovered. These cases are usually filed under seal, meaning they are confidential.

I would encourage anyone who wants to expose fraud to be patient with the process and hire an attorney who specializes in false claim cases. Keep good documentation, such as email, financial records, and names of all of those involved. The government will investigate and will decide whether to take the case or not. If you

---

1. Joel D. Hesch, *Whistleblowing: A Guide to Government Reward Programs (How to Collect Millions of Dollars for Reporting Fraud)* (Lynchburg, VA: Goshen Press, 2010).
2. "Justice Department's False Claims Act Settlements and Judgments Exceed \$5.6 Billion in Fiscal Year 2021," The United States Department of Justice, February 2, 2022, https://www.justice.gov/opa/pr/justice-department-s-false-claims-act-settlements-and-judgments-exceed-56-billion-fiscal-year.

know that fraud has definitely been committed, you will be rewarded for being true to what is right. You are helping the government combat fraud and hold those accountable for their actions.

If a provider is convicted of fraud, they may be put on the Medicare exclusion list and could be at risk of losing their license. An employer could face consequences if they hire someone who is on the Medicare exclusion list.[3]

The OIG also regulates corporate integrity agreements (CIA) with health care providers and other entities as part of the settlement of Federal Health Care Program investigations arising under a variety of civil false claim statutes. Providers or entities agree to the obligations, and in exchange, OIG agrees not to seek their exclusion from participation in Medicare, Medicaid, or other Federal health care programs. Always do the right thing; you never know how you will be rewarded.

---

3. Department of Health and Human Services Office of Inspector General, "Search the Exclusions Database," Search the Exclusions Database | Office of Inspector General, accessed January 16, 2023, https://exclusions.oig.hhs.gov/.

Discussion Questions

1. Does fraud affect everyone?

2. Would you risk your job to report fraud?

3. Would you be fearful of retaliation for reporting fraud?

4. What are some of the consequences of reporting fraud?

5. Did you know that you could be rewarded for reporting fraud?

6. Why is it important to be true to what is right?

7. Can you define some types of government fraud?

⁓ Notes for Discussion Questions ⁓

9

Give it Back and Pay it Forward

It is good to give back to someone who has given to you. A neighborhood grocery store we frequented often when I was growing up used to let my mom get food on credit. I now realize that was such a good deed, and I am now able to give to an organization that was started by the founder of the store. I am not only giving to that organization, but I am paying it forward to all those people that are now benefiting from that organization. I would like to share a letter that I wrote to that organization—The Manna House:

When the building the Manna House occupies used to be a grocery store owned by Nick and Olla Rae Chicola, I grew up in Alexandria Louisiana Sonia Quarters. I am the youngest of five children. Nick's Chicola grocery store was a staple in the community when I was growing up. I fondly remember Mrs. Nick (Olla Rae) as a very loving and kind lady. I grew up poor and I remember her letting my mother get groceries on credit at the store so that we could have food to eat to last us for the remainder of the month. My mother would pay Nick Chicola Grocery when she received her check. In 1990, Manna House opened in the same location as the old grocery store. My mother and sister were on a limited income and used to eat at the Manna House. I thought it was just a place for homeless people but realized later that it wasn't. My mother and sister told her the food was great and they knew others at the Manna House. One of my passions in life is to help those who are less fortunate in life for whatever reason that may be. Nick Chicola Grocery came to my family's rescue when we were in need. I am now blessed to be a blessing. I told my sister that I donated to the Manna House, and she said that was good and reminded me that the late Ms. Nick cared about people and was a blessing to many. I became compelled to donate regularly. Many people had it hard during the pandemic. The prices of food have gone up. I am grateful that I am in a position to pay it forward. I urge others to try to get on a system where they can regularly donate.

It's always good to pay it forward and do random acts of kindness. When I was at a fast-food restaurant in the drive through line earlier this year, I placed my order and when I got to the window, the cashier told me that someone had already paid for my food. I was astonished because I did not know what had happened. The cashier told me that the car before me had paid for my meal. I must admit, I did not know what that concept was all about. I blew my horn at the car ahead of me to acknowledge my gratefulness.

I told my husband about the incident, and he said that usually the gesture is to pay for the person's meal that was in the car behind me. I had never heard of that particular gesture in a fast-food line. I like to give to people and organizations. A lot of the organizations do charitable deeds all year long. There are people that do random acts of kindness all the time.

One definition of kindness is to be considerate. I was in a restaurant and an elderly man came in with a big dog. I looked around at the dog, and the server was polite and said, "He's a service dog."

I knew that; however, I was just looking at the dog to make sure that he was friendly. The gentleman turned around and asked me if I was okay with the dog sitting on the floor behind me. I said I was okay and thanked him for asking me. The dog was quiet the whole time that he was sitting behind me. It could have been a different story if we both were not considerate. It is not unusual now to see dogs in restaurants or on airplanes. Instead of thinking about "random" acts of kindness, it is good to be kind all the time. This gentleman made my day and I felt good about returning the gesture and letting him know that his dog was not an issue. Could you imagine how better off society would be if we all practiced being kind to one another? It states in the first part of Ephesian 4:32 "Be kind and compassionate to one another."

I grew up in poverty and appreciated the act of kindness that was shown toward me and my family. It sometimes seems hard to accept acts of kindness, but do not be embarrassed about it because I am sure the people feel good about giving.

Once, at a church that I attended, a lady gave me a check and told me to sign my name on it, she had filled out all the other information. I was so grateful for her act of kindness. We were talking about taking an upcoming layperson Bible class and the fee was $100. I must admit that I have paid for friends' dinners and given them money when I knew that they did not have any money. I know how to be receptive when someone gives something to me.

Benefits of Giving Back

One way to give back is by volunteering your time. Volunteers are important; think about the places or events that you go to every day that may have volunteers. There are volunteer firefighters, volunteers at hospitals, parades, and about any event you attend in your community. Volunteering your services is an effective way to network and gain valuable experience.

Acts 30:35 in the Bible states "it is more blessed to give than receive."

I know sometimes there are people who may try to exploit and take advantage of someone. However, if you can give to someone or do a random act of kindness, that in itself can be rewarding. It does not always have to be a monetary gesture. I recall a coworker of mine thanked me for my smile. I will never forget that. We would always just make little funny remarks to each other, and one particular day I was not having it and just gave her a big smile. She just looked at me and said, "By the way, thanks for the smile!"

That really made my day! Whether you bless someone with your finances, time, or smile, you never know how you could be giving back and paying it forward. When you do something from the heart – that is what really matters. Sometimes society glorifies acts of unkindness, but it's always good to do random acts of kindness throughout the year and not just during the holidays!

Discussion Questions

1. Have you ever received a random act of kindness?

2. What does paying it forward mean to you?

3. Do you feel guilty when someone does something nice for you? What could you do to accept it and allow them the benefits of giving?

4. Do you like it when someone demonstrates a random act of kindness toward you?

5. Do you like paying it forward?

Conclusion

"Remember ye not the former things, neither consider the things of old. Behold, I will do a new thing; now it shall spring forth; shall ye not know it? I will even make a way in the wilderness, and rivers in the desert." Isaiah 43:18-19

What the scriptures is saying is move on and let it go and God will make a way. I am looking forward to making room for more in the coming year!

My journey to living the abundant life has not been easy, but I am now reaping the fruits of my labor as are others who have helped me along the journey. Whatever it is you want in life, go after it. You will encounter some roadblocks and may have some limitations. I am here to tell you that roadblocks are temporary and necessary, but you will eventually go around them and through them if you do not give up. Go ahead and take some detours in life to get to your destination.

Surround yourself around positive people that will lift you up and not try to tear you down. Give yourself permission to give them the gift of goodbye. Goodbye has several definitions, so you get to decide what it means to you. It does not have to be a love/hate situation, it can just mean that you are moving on to a new level, and sometimes you have to let go to get to your destination in life.

I hope after reading this book you will be able to move on to a new level in life that makes you happy. I wish you Godspeed!

Acknowledgments

I would like to thank my family and friends who always encouraged me in life. I also would like to thank my husband Johnny for his unconditional love and support of me as I spent so much time on this new chapter of my life. Thank you for helping me with all of the drafts and proofreading. I would like to thank all of the people in my life that have encouraged me over the years, from ministers to co-workers, and teachers. A special thanks to all of my first readers.

I would like to thank Steve Harrison Team and all of the coaches that helped me to put this book together. A special thanks to Christy Day and Maggie McLaughlin of Constellation Book Services, Valerie Costa, Editor, Costa Creative Services, and Steve Scholl of The WaterStone Agency.

I want to thank God for blessing me to write "Living The Abundant Life" 9 steps to Move From Poverty to Prosperity. I thank you God for giving me the power to get wealth.

High School Picture

Sylvia and Aunt Gladys – Detroit Michigan

Undergraduate College Picture

Mr. and Mrs. O'Connor Wedding Photo

Young Adult Picture

Master's Degree Photo

Sylvia and Johnny Volunteer Event

Sylvia and Johnny Engagement Picture

Aunt Gladys and Sylvia – Mall Michigan

Johnny and Sylvia Wedding Photo

Johnny and Sylvia Holiday Photo 2022 picture 1

Sylvia and Johnny Holiday 2022 picture 2

Mrs. Sylvia O'Connor Holiday 2022 Picture 3

Mr. Johnny O'Connor

SYLVIA O'CONNOR has overcome poverty and has made it her mission to help others do the same. She moved to Detroit from her small southern town in Louisiana to seek a better life. There, she got an education and started pursuing and accomplishing her dreams and goals. Her past has never determined her future. Though she has had some bumps and bruises in life, she knows something about going beyond her comfort zone and experiencing what is on the other side of moving on.

O'Connor grew up in poverty in Southern Louisiana. Realizing she did not have a lot of positive role models to guide her, she contacted her aunt about moving to Detroit. Her first obstacle was that her aunt did not respond. O'Connor persisted and eventually received a one-way bus ticket, moved to Detroit, and attended college there. She later obtained a master's degree in administration from Central Michigan University and holds the following certifications: RHIA (Registered Health Information Administrator), CPMA (Certified Professional Medical Auditor, CCS (Certified Coding Specialist), and CRC (Certified Risk Coder). She became an adjunct professor in allied health at Davenport University at the Livonia, Warren, and Dearborn Campuses. She spent over thirty years working in health care where she became a whistleblower exposing health care fraud. A former volunteer at Woman's Hospital in Baton Rouge, Louisiana, O'Connor is currently an auxiliary member there.

Sylvia's faith in God helps sustain her, and her motto is "If you will believe in yourself, you can achieve your dreams and goals."

Sylvia O'Connor is the CEO of Sylvia O'Connor SOAR LLC. She now lives in the Baton Rouge area with her husband Johnny O'Connor, Sr.

https://sylvia-oconnor.com